MAXIMISING YOUR INTELLECTUAL ABILITIES

Learn how to make the most of your intelligence

Written by Maïlys Charlier

Translated by Jessica Foster

Coaching **50MINUTES**.com

MAXIMISING YOUR INTELLECTUAL ABILITIES

- **Issue:** which techniques will allow me to maximise my intellectual potential?
- **Uses:** being capable of using our brain's full capacity to work quickly and efficiently and to make the fewest mistakes possible.
- **Professional context:** career progression, acquiring a position of responsibility, team or project management, brainstorming, personal development, professional creativity.
- **FAQs:**
  - What behaviour do I need to adopt to look after my brain on a daily basis?
  - Why is it important to train my brain?
  - Why is it easier to learn when we are young?
  - Are brain-training games really effective?
  - Is it dangerous to resort to medication to improve my mental capacity if I am not suffering from any illness?
  - How long will it be before I notice an improvement in my intellectual capabilities?
  - Does my way of thinking depend on whether I prefer using the left or right hemisphere?

Human beings only use 10% of their brain capacity. Everyone is aware of this fact, but what does it really mean? This observation, attributed to Albert Einstein (German physicist, 1879-1955), is based on the fact that, even if we use all our neurones throughout the day, they are not active at the same time. Additionally, there are billions of possible connections between them.

Does that mean that it is possible to increase this percentage and develop our mental capacity? Can we reprogramme our brains, neutralise our mechanisms and change our way of making them work? This organ, which is not dissimilar to a computerised machine, works in a very complex way; scientists do not even (yet) know its limits. Indispensable to our daily lives, it allows us to memorise, learn, act, interpret, eat, breathe: in short, to live. Our brains are constantly adapting; they can change and remodel themselves at any age by creating new neurones, and constantly evolve based on our personal experiences.

In his work *Psycho-Cybernetics*, Maxwell Maltz (American doctor and author, 1899-1975) confirmed that the brain comprises a success mechanism which can be activated like a button to take full advantage of our capabilities and reach our objectives. As it works like a muscle, it is therefore only necessary to train this organ and maintain it to further our intelligence. The American William James (founder of modern psychology, 1842-1910) explains that "a human can alter his life by altering his attitude." How, then, can we develop this extra intelligence? What exercises and maintenance does our brain need to work optimally? How can we activate this success mechanism? In just 50 minutes, this booklet will guide you through the different steps to follow to maximise your intellectual capacity and use your mind to its full potential.

USING YOUR BRAIN TO YOUR ADVANTAGE: THE BASICS

DISCOVERING OUR OWN INTELLIGENCE

What do our brains consist of?

The brain is the central organ of the nervous system. Its job is to control our bodies' motor functions and ensure our cognitive functions. It is made up of two hemispheres:

- **The left hemisphere** controls language, as was discovered by Paul Broca (French neurologist, 1824-1880) in 1861. It is also responsible for logic, reasoning, arithmetic and intelligence.
- **The right hemisphere** manages spatial awareness, overall intelligence, intuition and artistic ability, as was demonstrated by Roger Wolcott Sperry (American neurophysiologist, 1913-1994) in the 1960s. This specialist notably proved that all new information passes through the right hemisphere. It is therefore through it that we learn, while the left hemisphere assimilates and stores information.

SOME OBSERVATIONS ABOUT THE BRAIN

- It is the best protected organ in the body thanks to the skull.
- In adults, it weighs more than a kilogramme.
- It is made up of between 86 and 100 billion nervous cells, called neurones.

- It is mostly fed by glucose and oxygen.
- It is 60% fat.
- Neurones communicate between each other via electrical signals thanks to the synapses (connection zone between neurones). These nerve impulses produce chemical substances known as neurotransmitters.

Neuroplasticity

Neuroplasticity means the capacity of our neurones to adapt to any change in their environment, whether that be changes in our internal organism or new external stimuli that have appeared in our lives. This ability is created by two processes: the creation of new neurones (neurogenesis) and the removal of inefficient or less useful connections (synaptic pruning) which allows the others to be reinforced.

Throughout our lives, we acquire beliefs and ideas which, through repetition, produce neurone connections. These are strengthened while the information is reproduced. This is what creates our mental programming. To change it, we need to break our habits and change our beliefs. The brain is therefore capable of creating or reorganising neurones and the connections between them in accordance with our emotional, physical and cognitive experiences. Nonetheless, it is not that simple, because these thoughts are complex and are the result of a number of different elements (sight, smell, sound, taste, emotion, atmosphere, etc.). This cerebral plasticity is more naturally developed in childhood than in adulthood, although it is still possible as long as we train our brains with different exercises and adopt appropriate behaviours.

REPROGRAMMING OUR BRAINS

The brain is made up of different parts: the conscious, the preconscious (which links the conscious and the unconscious), the unconscious and the subconscious. The latter registers the information we receive and the experiences we have. Unlike the conscious mind, which is linked to a controlled mental activity, the subconscious is linked to uncontrolled mental activity, within the unconscious. These four parts are closely linked and act upon one another. With the information gathered daily by the conscious, the subconscious shapes our habits, our reflexes, our fears and our beliefs. It is what programmes our brain through our thoughts.

Sylvain Wealth confirms this himself in his article *A year to reprogramme my brain*: "thoughts lead to actions and actions create habits"[1]. Although habits are extremely useful in everyday life, they sometimes influence our brains in a negative way according to our experiences, and can block the positive development of our intellect. Thus, a better use of our mental capacity can be achieved partly by changing our way of thinking and by 'reprogramming' our subconscious to an approach of fulfilment and therefore of success.

---

1. This quotation has been translated by 50Minutes.com.

Reprogramming techniques

- **Creative visualisation:** when a challenge, a task or an important meeting is ahead of you, mentally visualise the objectives that you would like to reach. Do this preferably just before you go to sleep. Imagine that you are your future self and let yourself be taken over by the positive emotions that you feel while doing this. This exercise will help you to get rid of negative thoughts and get closer to achieving your objectives.

- **Positive affirmation:** to make sure every chance is on your side and to begin the day well, start by repeating several positive phrases out loud: "I am extraordinary", "I am a leader" or "I will manage it". Through this process, you will rebuild your confidence and programme your subconscious for success. This also works with your work environment: decorate it and arrange it in a positive way by displaying phrases or photos that motivate you.

- **Hypnosis and EMDR (Eye Movement Desensitisation and Reprocessing):** these techniques will allow you to unconsciously unblock a traumatic memory and resolve it so that you can move on.

EMDR

Eye Movement Desensitisation and Reprocessing, which depends on eye movement to heal the mind, was developed by the American psychologist Francine Shapiro (born in 1948) in the 1980s. This theory is based on the realisation that talking is generally not enough to liberate oneself from trauma. We need to appeal to all our channels of representation (perceptions, cognitions, emotions, bodily sensations) to re-access that traumatic memory in order to change our relationship to it. To do this, a sensory stimulus such as eye movement can be very beneficial for the creation of new connections which replace the traumatic feeling with calmer emotions.

- **Cognitive behavioural therapy:** each kind of therapy has its own techniques, but they all have the same objective, which is to reset our brains to new bases. These treatments depend on correcting negative thoughts and learning suitable behaviours.
- **Subliminal programming:** this involves regularly listening to audio recordings with subliminal messages which directly address the subconscious.
- **Autosuggestion:** this is not only based on phrases to repeat on a loop to reach your objective, but also – and in fact mainly – on the attitude adopted to do so. Thus, if you are trying to be confident, start by adopting the appropriate posture and tone of voice.
- **Self-hypnosis:** before entering into a hypnotic state, concentrate on your breathing, relax and repeat a positive autosuggestion phrase that is linked to your objectives. This will remain in your subconscious during the exercise.
- **'Reframing':** everyone has their own concept of reality depending on their perceptions, experiences, self-esteem and self-confidence. When an event occurs in someone's life, it is interpreted according to their vision of reality. The idea of 'reframing' involves deciphering these events

outside of their particular setting, by taking maximum distance from them and taking the information that is not linked to the person concerned into account. By giving a new version to their reality, the person will be more positive and open to external events as well as to the people around them. By using this technique, we reprogramme our brains, which allows us to better use our mental capacity.

Mental limitations

Mental limitations or limiting thoughts are obstacles that we impose consciously or unconsciously: "I can't apply to that job, I'm not good enough for it", "I will never manage to learn a new language, I'm not clever enough", etc. These beliefs, which we assimilate to truths, come from personal experiences, family or society. Thus, to help our brains evolve, it is important to get rid of these mental limitations, which slow down intellectual development. To do this, we must all eliminate these restrictions that are rooted deep within us, using opposing affirmations such as: "I am good enough to do that job" or "I have all the required qualities for this job". The more you repeat these affirmations, the more you will overcome the blockages that are keeping you from your objective.

NLP

The beliefs that we accumulate based on our experiences influence our way of thinking and behaving. Nonetheless, it is possible to consciously use this material stored in our brains. Within this context, the Americans John Grinder (linguist, born 1940) and Richard Brandler (psychologist, born 1950) created neuro-linguistic programming, which aims to understand communication between people as well as the relationship between language and thought. NLP allows individuals, among other things, to identify what is holding them back and to modify their beliefs to help themselves to improve.

Brain gymnastics

The brain is like a muscle: it must be trained to improve its capabilities. Thus, the key is continued learning. Acquiring new knowledge allow us to create new synaptic connections and reinforce those that already exist. According to Donald Hebb (Canadian neuropsychologist, 1904-1985), the more our neurones are activated, the more easily they connect to one another. Learning thus becomes automatic and requires less effort on our part. This is notably the case when we begin learning a language: the more we speak, the easier it becomes to express ourselves. On the other hand, if we do not practice, the synaptic connections get weaker, in the same way as our muscles if we do not exercise, and we forget what we have acquired.

Memory is indispensable in every learning process (a sport, a musical instrument, a language, etc.) as it allows us to store information and recall it later. There are three types of memory:

- **Sensory memory** deals with all the information that reaches us daily through our five senses. This data is stored for a very short amount of time (a few seconds) and is sent to the short-term memory if we believe it is relevant.
- **Short term memory** registers a limited quantity of information which is stored for a restricted period of time (less than one minute).

- **Long term memory** stores the important events in our lives and acts as our reserve of knowledge. It is unlimited, but unfortunately not infallible.

Try to do mental gymnastics for several minutes every day to develop your abilities. Stimulate your immediate memory by learning an extract from a poem, some quotes or simply a telephone number by using mnemonic techniques. Exercise your capacity for observation by mentally reproducing a chart, a photo or a scene that you have already seen. Finally, work on your logic by completing a number series or doing Sudokus. Thanks to this brain gymnastics, your brain will become more active.

A suitable diet

Our brain uses 15-20% of our energy every day. To work correctly, it therefore needs specific nutrients. A varied and balanced diet constitutes one of the bases for the development of our mental capacity. Thus, the optimal foods are listed below.

- **Foods with a low glycaemic index (GI)** provide the

necessary energy to get through the day thanks to their glucose content. These are most fruits, vegetables and whole grains.

- **Dairy products** give us the necessary proteins for our brains to work, but also vitamins B2 and B12, which are vital to intellectual development.
- **Berries** (blackberries, blueberries, raspberries, currants, etc.) **and citrus fruits** (lemons, grapefruits, oranges, etc.) are rich in antioxidants which slow down the ageing of the brain.
- **Foods rich in vitamins B6 and B9** eliminate homocysteine, an amino acid which is poisonous to neurones. They are notably present in offal, pulses and dark green leafy vegetables.
- **Avocado**, rich in vitamin E, dilates blood vessels and thus improves blood circulation.
- **Eggs** contain many A, D and E vitamins as well as B vitamins (B2, B5, B9 or folic acid, B12), but also choline, which helps cerebral development.
- **Broccoli and spinach** contain vitamin K, which is essential to the functioning of the cerebral system.
- **Fatty acids and Omega 3,** which are notably present in fish, improve the brain's cognitive functions.
- **Green tea,** which produces dopamine, is beneficial to memory and decreases cerebral fatigue.
- **Natural spices** such as ginseng, hypericum, turmeric and gingko, as well as some fine herbs such as sage or rosemary, stimulate our cerebral capabilities, including memory, concentration and learning.

Regular exercise also boosts the brain's capabilities. Indeed, physical activity accelerates blood flow to the brain, thus increasing the supply of oxygen and glucose. Sport also leads to the release of a substance called "Brain-Derived Neurotrophic Factor" (BDNF), which creates and preserves neurones.

On the other hand, the following foods are not recommended, either generally or following a conscious decision to improve your intellect.

- **Saturated fats,** which can be found in products such as fried food, cooked meats or crisps, should be avoided, as they destroy nerve cells. Consequently, you should avoid very fatty meals such as fast food which reduce your levels of dopamine, a substance that is responsible for your feeling of well-being.
- **Refined sugars** (corn syrup, white and brown cane sugar, fructose), which are present in soda and factory-produced fruit juice, have no nutritional value, slow down the brain and can lead to memory problems. Opt for raw sugar or honey instead.
- Similarly, **artificial sweeteners,** such as aspartame, can lead to brain damage. Instead, eat moderate quantities of unrefined sugar.
- **Pesticides,** present in fruit and vegetables, are also dangerous for your brain and the rest of your body. Always remember to wash fruit and vegetables thoroughly

before eating them. You can even soak them in water for a few minutes in order to get rid of these chemical substances.

- **Alcohol** impairs our judgement and leads to memory problems.
- **Tobacco** is not only harmful to your lungs, but also to your brain.

Meditation vs. stress

The accumulation of stress and fatigue are harmful to your neurones and your memory. Additionally, tension can have a negative impact on language and thought. You must therefore remain attentive to this. If you notice memory loss or significant instances of forgetting things, check you are sleeping enough and that you are not anxious or stressed about one thing in particular.

A simple and accessible way to fix this state and to make the best use of your intellectual abilities is meditation. Not only will anxiety and stress decrease while sleep and concentration improve, but additionally, meditation activates the left pre-frontal cortex, which is linked to positive emotions. According to the American psychologist Daniel Goleman (born 1946), meditation is a way of training the brain, and is also capable of deconditioning innate reflexes. In 1998, another American, Paul Ekman (born 1934) carried out an experiment with a Buddhist monk: in the middle of meditation, the professor tried to make him jump with a deafening sound; the monk did not move a muscle or even bat an eyelid. The experiment illustrated the extent to which meditation can allow an individual to master their mind.

Medication

There are stimulants that can influence our intellectual abilities. These drugs produce neurotransmitters (dopamine and serotonin) which directly act on memory and blood circulation.

- Generally used to assuage concentration problems, Ritaline and Adderal improve concentration and allow information to be better assimilated.
- Modafinil is prescribed as treatment for narcolepsy. This medication stimulates the secretion of histamine, a neurotransmitter that causes alertness. However, a lack of sleep still prevents effective assimilation of information.
- Developed in 1959, centrophenoxine increases the flow of oxygen and glucose to the brain, thus stimulating cerebral functions. It also has antioxidant properties.
- Nootropics or 'smart drugs', such as DMAE, are substances aimed at improving cognitive performance and in theory cause no or very few harmful effects. They can be simple dietary supplements (choline, tyrosine), drugs, plants (theanine, water hyssop) or molecules.

Be careful! Do not put your health at risk and always consult a doctor before taking these drugs, particularly as most of them require a prescription. Several schools and some specialists are more resistant than others when it comes to using this type of medication. Do not forget that every type of medication can have side effects. Make sure you have consulted your GP and carefully read the instructions and precautions before taking anything.

TOP TIPS

- **Work on the speed of your mind.** Current technology has made us become accustomed to no longer relying on our memories and intellectual abilities. Phones with calculators and electronic calendars, GPS, computers, online encyclopaedias and online translators are enemies of our brains. These tools make it lazy, without even taking into account the stress they can lead to.
- **Set yourself precise and realistic objectives.** Do not set the bar too high at the beginning: your objective should be appropriate for your current abilities, or you risk quickly becoming discouraged. Gradually increase the level of difficulty by doubling a task or reducing the time you take to do it, for example.
- **Ask yourself the right questions.** Your brain responds to every question you think of, even if it is completely irrelevant. It is therefore important to ask yourself questions about what really counts, in the most positive way possible. Thus, do not ask yourself why you are failing, but rather what you can do to succeed.
- **Escape your routine.** This will help you to keep up your interest and therefore your concentration. Additionally, in this way you will prevent your brain from going into autopilot by making it work.
- **Train yourself to do several things at the same time.** Working on different tasks at the same time will get your short-term memory working. Start with habitual, simple tasks. These short exercises will force you to meet different challenges.

- **Think positive thoughts.** The more positive and enthusiastic thoughts you have, the more your objective will be etched into your subconscious.
- **Play!** If learning is somewhat difficult for you, train your mind with playful exercises. In this way you will develop your intellectual abilities without forcing yourself. Brainteasers, Sudokus, card games for when you are alone; Risk, Monopoly, Connect 4, chess, among others for when you are in a group...it's up to you to find the game that best suits your intelligence.

FAQS

Some simple actions will allow you to take care of your brain:

- Eating healthily is essential, but it is also important not to neglect certain foods which encourage the brain to work well, such as Omega 3, which can be found in nuts (almonds, walnuts and hazelnuts) for example, and Omega 6, which is found in particular in vegetable oil and grains.
- Continue to learn, as the more we learn, the easier it is.
- Use your brain as much as possible: forget your phone calculator, electronic diary and GPS. Make the most of your memory, use mental arithmetic and trust your sense of direction.
- Get enough sleep. A minimum of seven hours a night is necessary for a healthy brain.
- Drink at least 1.5 litres of water a day, more if you exercise or if it is hot. Being well-hydrated is necessary for the brain's neurological activity.
- Make sure you are getting enough antioxidants. These lead to increased oxygen flow to the brain and slow down its ageing process.

WHY IS IT EASIER TO LEARN WHEN WE ARE YOUNG?

When we are young, our synaptic connections are greater in number, and faster. Additionally, our subconscious has not yet fixed limiting thoughts. There are therefore almost no obstacles to integrating new information. Moreover, our concentration and memory are also more reliable.

WHY IS IT IMPORTANT TO TRAIN MY BRAIN?

The brain is like a muscle: we therefore need to train it so that we do not lose anything we have learnt. Indeed, if you stop practising a language, for example, you will forget it. It is thus necessary to regularly use your brain by practising it. Brain training also allows our synaptic connections to remain active, which allows the neurones to react more easily and quickly.

ARE BRAIN-TRAINING GAMES REALLY EFFECTIVE?

Brain-training games such as Brain Gym or mind mapping are effective, as they improve communication between the two hemispheres of the brain. This facilitates learning and exercises the brain. It will then have greater plasticity and your mental capabilities will be optimised.

IS IT DANGEROUS TO RESORT TO MEDICATION TO IMPROVE MY MENTAL CAPACITY IF I AM NOT SUFFERING FROM ANY ILLNESS?

Only take medication if your doctor advises you to and if you have a problem with your intellectual faculties (concentration, memory, etc.). If the medication is approved, there will be no or very little danger. However, make sure you read the warnings and keep an eye out for any potential side effects.

HOW LONG WILL IT BE BEFORE I NOTICE AN IMPROVEMENT IN MY INTELLECTUAL CAPABILITIES?

Similarly to when we are training, one session of exercise is not enough to see encouraging results. Be patient: the brain works like a muscle, and so you will be able to see improvements after a few weeks or months of doing the exercises.

DOES MY WAY OF THINKING DEPEND ON WHETHER I PREFER USING THE LEFT OR RIGHT HEMISPHERE?

Most people more naturally use the left hemisphere of their brains, the language side. However, when instinct and emotions are at play, the right hemisphere is the active one. Consequently, more emotional and instinctive people tend to use their right hemisphere; they do not follow the same intelligence or logic as the people who use the other half of the brain.

OVER TO YOU

MIND MAPPING

This exercise involves associating ideas in the form of a tree shape. In the centre, write a word or draw a small picture and link as many ideas as possible with it. Use a different colour and size for each thought. The aim is to create as many connections as possible and use your creativity. The main advantage of mind mapping is that it encourages communication between the two hemispheres of the brain: words and their arrangement concern the left hemisphere while colours, pictures and an overall view of the topic draw on the right side.

BRAIN GYM

Created by the education professional Paul Dennison, Brain Gym offers exercises for developing our learning capabilities. Train your brain with the help of a few simple exercises!

- Walk on the spot, touching your left knee with your right hand and vice versa. This leads to better exchange between the two hemispheres.
- Drawing the infinity sign with your eyes boosts concentration and memorising.
- Cross your ankles and wrists and interlock your fingers. This cross contact increases our capacity for attention and listening.

VISUALISE YOUR SUCCESS

Imagine in your mind that you are reaching your objectives, as if you were there. With a small amount of training, your brain will see no difference between this film and reality and will therefore be positively conditioned. Thus, the day before your first day in a new job or an important meeting, replay the positive little film of this moment in your head, thinking about the details (sounds, colours, images, smells, emotions). Your mind will be conditioned so that the day unfolds as you have imagined. Have confidence in yourself and ensure that all the odds are in your favour.

We want to hear from you!
Leave a comment on your online library
and share your favourite books on social media!

FURTHER READING

BIBLIOGRAPHY

- Agid, Y. (2014) Comprendre le cerveau et son fonctionnement. *ICM*. [Online]. [Accessed 4 October 2015]. Available from: <http://icm-institute.org/fr/actualite/comprendre-le-cerveau-et-son-fonctionnement/>
- Allodocteurs (2014) *Renforcer son mental pour se dépasser.* [Online]. [Accessed 19 September 2015]. Available from: <http://www.allodocteurs.fr/actualite-sante-renforcer-son-mentalpour-se-depasser_13738.html>
- Bandler, R. and Grinder, J. (1975) *The Structure of Magic: A Book About Language and Therapy.* Palo Alto: Science & Behavior Books.
- Bartczak, S. (2013) Utilisons-nous seulement 10 % de notre cerveau?. *Le Point.* [Online]. [Accessed 12 October 2015]. Available from: <http://www.lepoint.fr/sante/utilisons-nous-seulement-10-denotre-cerveau-29-03-2013-1647342_40.php>
- Césaire, J. (No date). Quatre techniques pour exploiter la magnifique puissance de votre subconscient. *Le blog des méthodes douces.* [Online]. [Accessed 19 September 2015]. Available from: <http://methodes-douces-et-bien-etre.com/epanouissement-personnel-3/4-techniques-pour-exploiter-la-magnifique-puissance-de-votre-subconscient/>
- Christine, M. (No date). Comment utiliser le pouvoir de nos cerveaux droit et gauche pour un résultat maximum. *Vivre ses talents.* [Online]. [Accessed 19 September 2015]. Available from: <http://www.vivresestalents.fr/mental/

comment-utiliser-le-pouvoir-de-nos-cerveaux-droit-et-gauche-pour-un-resultat-maximum/>
- Dalla Costa, V. (No date). Préparation mentale : comment atteindre ses objectifs ?. *Nutri-site*. [Online]. [Accessed 19 September 2015] Available from: <http://www.nutri-site.com/dossier-entrainement--preparation-mentale-atteindre-objectifs-sportif--2--230.html>
- Ferrari, M. (2013) Cinq techniques pour dépasser vos limitations mentales tout de suite. *Esprit riche*. [Online]. [Accessed 19 September 2015]. Available from: <http://esprit-riche.com/5-techniques-pour-depasser-vos-limitations-mentales-tout-de-suite/>
- Gannac, A.-L. (2008) Êtes-vous plutôt cerveau gauche ou cerveau droit?. *Psychologies*. [Online]. [Accessed 6 October 2015]. Available from: <http://test.psychologies.com/tests-psycho/tests-memoire-et-cerveau/Etes-vous-cerveau-droit-ou-cerveau-gauche>
- Garteiser, M. (2015) Fumer: moins de QI et des risques de maladie d'Alzheimer. *e-santé*. [Online]. [Accessed 30 October 2015]. Available from: <http://www.e-sante.be/fumer-moins-qi-risques-alzheimer/actualite/470>
- Green, C. and Bavelier, D. (2003) Action Video Game Modifies Visual Selective Attention. *Nature*. 423, pp. 534-537.
- Hodent-Villaman, C. (2012) Les jeux vidéo sont-ils bons pour le cerveau ?. *Sciences humaines*. [Online]. [Accessed 30 October 2015]. Available from: <http://www.scienceshumaines.com/les-jeux-video-sont-ils-bonspour-le-cerveau_fr_15191.html>
- Hug, H. (2013) PNL : comment déprogrammer, reprogrammer votre cerveau ?. *Dimension*

- *Phoenix*. [Online]. [Accessed 4 October 2015].
  Available from: <http://dimension-phoenix.fr/
  pnl-deprogrammer-reprogrammer/>
- Maltz, M. (1960) *Psycho-Cybernetics: The Original Science
  of Self Improvement and Success That Has Changed the
  Lives of 30 Million People*. New York: Prentice Hall.
- Nutra News (2015) *La Centrophénoxine stimule le cerveau
  et lutte contre son vieillissement.* [Online]. [Accessed
  4 October 2015]. Available from:<http://www.
  nutranews.org/sujet.pl?id=415>
- Passeport santé (2009) *Une pilule pour stimuler le cerveau
  des gens en bonne santé ?* [Online]. [Accessed 4 October
  2015]. Available from: <http://www.passeportsante.net/
  fr/Communaute/Blogue/Fiche.aspx?doc=une-pilule-
  pour-stimuler-le-cerveau-des-gens-en-bonne-sante>
- Prigent, A. (2015) Changer de mode de vie pour protéger
  son cerveau. *Le Figaro*. [Online]. [Accessed 4 October
  2015]. Available from: <http://sante.lefigaro.fr/
  actualite/2015/03/27/23561-changer-mode-vie-pour-
  proteger-son-cerveau>
- Rhumatologie en pratique (2013) *Y a-t-il des moyens
  efficaces d'augmenter ses performances intellectuelles
  pour un examen?* [Online]. [Accessed 19 September
  2015]. Available from: <http://www.rhumatopratique.
  com/wp/rp/2013/05/15/y-a-t-il-des-moyens-efficaces-
  daugmenter-ses-performances-intellectuelles-pour-un-
  examen-2/>
- Rogelet, A. (2004) Comment muscler son cerveau.
  Psychologies. [Online]. [Accessed 19 September 2015].
  Available from: <http://www.psychologies.com/Bien-
  etre/Prevention/Hygiene-de-vie/Articles-et-Dossiers/

Comment-muscler-son-cerveau>

- Soleille, C. (2014) Quatre moyens originaux pour booster son cerveau. *La nutrition.* [Online]. [Accessed 19 September 2015]. Available from: <https://www.lanutrition.fr/bien-dans-son-assiette/bien-dans-son-age/pendant%20les%20examens/comment-manger-pendant-les-exams-/4-moyens-originaux-pour-booster-son-cerveau>
- Surpassez-vous (No date). *Comment la neuroplasticité peut changer votre vie.* [Online]. [Accessed 4 October 2015]. Available from: <http://www.surpassez-vous.com/la-pensee-positive/laneuroplasticite-changer-votre-vie/>
- Wealth, S. (2013) Cinq façons d'augmenter la rapidité et la puissance de votre cerveau. *Sylvain Wealth.* [Online]. [Accessed 19 September 2015]. Available from: <http://www.sylvainwealth.com/5-facons-daugmenter-la-rapidite-et-la-puissance-de-votre-cerveau.html>
- Wealth, S. (2013) Je me suis donné 1 an pour reprogrammer mon cerveau. *Sylvain Wealth.* [Online]. [Accessed 19 September 2015]. Available from: <http://www.sylvainwealth.com/reprogrammer-son-cerveau.html>
- Ybarra, M. L., Diener-West, M., Markow, D., Leaf, P. J., Hamburger, M. and Boxer, P. (2008) Linkages Between Internet and Other Media Violence With Seriously Violent Behavior by Youth. *Pediatrics*, 122 (5), pp. 929-937.

ADDITIONAL SOURCES

- Dennison, P. and Dennison, G. (1992) *Brain Gym: Simple Activities for Whole Brain Learning*. California: Edu-Kinesthetics Inc.
- Hart, J. (2016) *The Brain Book: Understanding How the Brain Works and How to Improve Brain Performance*. London: New Holland Publishers.
- Kawashima, R. (2005) *Train Your Brain: 60 Days to a Better Brain*. New Jersey: Kumon Publishing.

IMPROVE YOUR GENERAL KNOWLEDGE

IN A BLINK OF AN EYE !

www.50minutes.com

www.50minutes.com

Ebook EAN: 9782806288905

Paperback EAN: 9782806288912

Legal Deposit: D/2016/12603/728

Cover: © Primento

Digital conception by Primento, the digital partner of publishers.

Made in the USA
Monee, IL
07 July 2026